FOLLOWING DIRECTIONS

REVISED!

NANCY LOBB

J. WESTON
WALCH
PUBLISHER
Portland, Maine

D1205553

User's Guide
to
Walch Reproducible Books

As part of our general effort to provide educational materials that are as practical and economical as possible, we have designated this publication a "reproducible book." The designation means that purchase of the book includes purchase of the right to limited reproduction of all pages on which this symbol appears:

Here is the basic Walch policy: We grant to individual purchasers of this book the right to make sufficient copies of reproducible pages for use by all students of a single teacher. This permission is limited to a single teacher and does not apply to entire schools or school systems, so institutions purchasing the book should pass the permission on to a single teacher. Copying of the book or its parts for resale is prohibited.

Any questions regarding this policy or requests to purchase further reproduction rights should be addressed to:

Permissions Editor
J. Weston Walch, Publisher
321 Valley Street • P. O. Box 658
Portland, Maine 04104-0658

1   2   3   4   5   6   7   8   9   10

ISBN 0-8251-3884-1

Copyright © 1985, 1999
J. Weston Walch, Publisher
P. O. Box 658 • Portland, Maine 04104-0658

Printed in the United States of America

CONTENTS

Part One: FOLLOWING ORAL DIRECTIONS

Part Two: FOLLOWING WRITTEN DIRECTIONS

TO THE TEACHER

How to Use This Book

Following Directions is a reproducible workbook containing both student and teacher material. The teacher material includes vocabulary, an answer key, and information pertaining to the student material that follows it. The student material contains exercises and some short reading selections.

Following Directions is divided into two parts: Following Oral Directions and Following Written Directions. These two areas involve different skills and different learning processes. Students will learn various techniques for improving both skills.

Students in English, reading, or special education classes will especially benefit from these exercises as they improve their skills in following many kinds of directions. In fact, this publication will be helpful for any students who need to improve their ability to listen and follow instructions.

Reproducible pages are identified by the Walch copyright line and "flame" logo at the bottom of each page. This material can be copied and distributed to each student.

Instructions

Pass out copies of pages *v* and *vi*, the Introduction. Students can read the pages and write their paragraph independently. Or, students can read the material as a class, discussing the writing assignment before completing it on their own.

Vocabulary

oral   maze   interchange   crisscross

Answer Key

Answers will vary.

Name _____ Date _____

Introduction

A man traveled to Dallas, Texas all the way from Anchorage, Alaska. It was an interesting trip. He had no trouble following the maze of highways on his maps.

But once he entered Dallas' bustling interchange of freeways, he couldn't remember the directions his friend had given him to get to his apartment.

He did remember the address. So, he stopped at a gas station to get directions. But, once again he forgot the directions. "Let's see. Did he say to turn right on Forrest, or was it left?" Unable to be sure, he once again was forced to stop for directions.

It was getting late. He knew he had crisscrossed Dallas several times. Finally, he gave up and phoned his friend to come get him. His amazed friend said, "Why, you've been going in circles all afternoon. You're only half a block from my place right now!"

Many people have trouble following directions. Yet, it's a skill we need again and again. Here are a few examples.

In school or on the job:

- following a teacher's oral directions
- following directions on a worksheet or test
- following directions on a homework assignment
- carrying out the boss's instructions

In everyday life:

- following directions on product labels
- following directions in a recipe
- following directions for using equipment
- following directions for locating a place

We all follow directions many times each day. By improving our skill at following directions, we can make life easier for ourselves.

(continued)

v   *Following Directions*

Introduction *(continued)*

In *Following Directions*, we've divided our study of following directions into two parts.

Part One

In Part One, you'll learn about following oral directions. Oral (spoken) directions are directions that you hear. You are getting oral directions when the teacher gives an assignment, when a friend tells you how to get to his house, or when your boss tells you how to do a job.

Part Two

In Part Two, you'll learn about following written instructions. You follow written instructions when you take a test, read a medicine label, or follow a cake recipe.

By the time you finish *Following Directions*, you'll be able to follow both oral and written directions better. You may find your grades will improve. People may think you listen better. And, you'll find it easier to try new things that require following directions to learn. So, let's get started.

Directions: In the space on the back of this sheet, write about a time when you didn't follow directions. Tell what happened as a result. Tell what you did differently the next time (or could do differently) to avoid the problem.

Part One

FOLLOWING ORAL DIRECTIONS

LISTENING VERSUS HEARING

Overview

The words *hearing* and *listening* are often used as synonyms in everyday language. However, they have quite different meanings in practice.

Hearing is the physical act of receiving sound through the ears. Sound waves enter the ears, and the brain tells us what we have heard. Hearing is an involuntary process which goes on even when we are asleep.

Listening, on the other hand, is a choice. We choose to listen to sounds which have meaning for us. We hear many sounds around us at all times. From those, we choose what we want to listen to.

The first step in following oral directions is to choose to listen to what is being said. We must pay attention in order to truly listen.

Sometimes, emotions can get in the way of listening. Anger, fear, or sadness can keep us from paying attention to what is being said. In these cases, we may not accurately listen to the message.

Instructions

Tell students that before you can follow spoken directions, you must first learn to listen to them. That sounds simple enough, because we listen all day long. Or, do we really?

Tell students that they are going to take a listening test. They are to sit quietly and listen for about 5 minutes. Afterwards, they will answer some questions.

When the 5 minutes are up, pass out Exercise 1. Have students complete questions 1–5.

Then try the experiment again. This time, the students are to keep their eyes closed as they listen for 5 minutes. When the time is up, have them answer questions 6 and 7, then read the information at the bottom of the page.

Vocabulary

hearing • listening • physical

Answer Key

1–4. Answers will vary.

5. Many students will find that their minds wandered during the 5 minutes. We all daydream. Without one thing to focus attention on, it is easy to let one's mind wander.

6. Students may find it easier to listen with their eyes open. That is because the eyes give us additional information about what is being heard. Some people say they can listen better when they are wearing their glasses or when they are close enough to a speaker to see him or her well.

7. The experiments show how many sounds go on around us all the time to which we do not really listen. We hear them, but do not pay attention to them.

Additional Activities

1. As a class, make a list of reasons students would choose to listen to (as opposed to merely hear) a verbal message. Answers could include:
   • The information is important for getting a good grade.

- The student is interested in what is being said.
- The student finds the speaker interesting.

2. Discuss instances in which students have heard, but not listened to, important information.

3. Discuss the effects daydreaming can have on listening. Discuss ways to control daydreaming.

4. Discuss the importance of eliminating distractions from the background when one is trying to pay attention to important information—for example, when studying.

5. Discuss the effect a hearing impairment would have on one's ability to listen.

LISTENING VERSUS HEARING

Try this listening test. Sit quietly. Listen for about 5 minutes. Then answer the questions below.

1. What was the loudest sound you heard?

   _____

2. What was the softest sound?

   _____

3. Did you hear any machinery being used? If so, what?

   _____

   _____

4. Did you hear anyone talking? If so, what were they talking about?

   _____

   _____

5. Did your mind wander during the 5-minute listening period? If so, why?

   _____

   _____

6. Try the experiment again. This time, keep your eyes closed as you listen for 5 minutes. What differences did you find?

   _____

   _____

7. What do you think these experiments show?

   _____

   _____

There are many sounds going on around us all the time. Our ears *hear* these sounds, but we don't pay attention to all of them. Therefore, we do not really *listen* to them.

Hearing is the physical act of receiving sound through the ears. But **listening** requires you to pay attention to what you hear. Listening begins with hearing, but listening takes place when we choose to pay attention to sounds that we find important.

ARE YOU A GOOD LISTENER?

Overview

Most people think they are good listeners. Yet, research has shown that most people listen at only a 25-percent efficiency level. Most of us have a variety of bad listening habits, such as allowing our minds to wander, interrupting, and jumping to conclusions.

Research also has shown that there are four key elements to good listening. They are hearing what is said, understanding its meaning, evaluating the message, and making a response.

1. Hearing what is said begins with the physical act of hearing. Listening requires paying attention and choosing what is important to us.

2. Understanding what is said involves interpreting the meaning of the speaker. A message involves more than just words. The speaker's tone of voice and body language add to the meaning of the words.

3. Evaluating what is said means thinking about what you hear, asking questions about what you don't understand, and coming to a thoughtful conclusion about what was said.

4. Your response to what was said shows that you heard and understood the message.

In Exercise 2, students have a chance to rate their listening habits. Being aware of possible problem areas is the first step in making any needed improvements.

Instructions

Discuss the advantages of being a better listener—for example, better grades, promotions on the job, people who like to talk to you, and making friends easier. Tell students they are going to complete a checklist of their own listening habits. Explain that there are no right or wrong answers. The purpose of the exercise is to help students look at their own listening habits and see areas of strength or weakness. Remind them that answering the questions honestly will help them learn something about themselves.

Discuss the four elements of good listening (detailed in the overview above) with the class.

Vocabulary

- eye contact
- interrupting
- mannerisms
- fidgeting

Answer Key

Answers will vary.

Additional Activities

1. Have students make a list of their best listening habits.

2. Have students list their worst listening habits. Ask them to make a plan for improving these habits.

3. Ask students to write a paragraph describing the listening behavior of a person they know who is a poor listener. Have them tell why this person is a poor listener. The students should not mention by name the poor listener they write about.

4. Have students write a paragraph telling about someone they know who is a good listener. They should explain why the person is a good listener and tell how it makes them feel to talk to the person.

5. Have students discuss how they feel when people do not listen to them.

6. Make a list of mannerisms that could get in the way of good listening. Examples include frowning, biting your lip, playing with your hair or clothing, and fidgeting.

7. Make a list of ways to look as if you are paying attention to a speaker. Examples include sitting up straight, looking alert, nodding or smiling appropriately as the person speaks, and making eye contact.

Name _____ Date _____

ARE YOU A GOOD LISTENER?

The first step in learning to follow oral directions is learning to be a better listener. Think about your listening habits.

Below are some good listening habits. Put an X in the box that best describes how often the statement applies to you when you are listening to another person.

	Often	Sometimes	Rarely
1. I make eye contact with the person speaking to me.			
2. I ask questions if I don't understand what's being said.			
3. I pay attention to the speaker.			
4. I listen for the main ideas of what's being said.			
5. I take notes if there are many details I should remember.			
6. I look interested.			
7. I avoid interrupting the speaker.			
8. I sit or stand still and avoid fidgeting or other mannerisms.			
9. I avoid finishing other people's sentences for them.			
10. I control my emotions and listen to the message.			
11. I react to what is being said with a smile or nod when it is appropriate.			
12. I listen to all the information before I make conclusions.			
13. I avoid letting my mind wander while the other person speaks.			
14. I focus on the speaker instead of on myself.			

7   *Following Directions*

LISTEN AND FOLLOW DIRECTIONS

Instructions

Give each student a copy of Exercise 3. Make sure that each student has a pencil (not a pen). Instruct them that in this exercise they are to follow the directions which you will read aloud. They are to blacken the boxes completely but not heavily. (Heavy marks will make it difficult to erase if need be.)

Read the following directions aloud to the students. Caution them to follow each direction carefully and exactly.

Find row 1 on your paper. Blacken the boxes in row 1 that contain names of kinds of cars. *(At this point, stop and check that students are blackening the boxes in the correct manner.)*

Blacken the boxes in row 2 that contain names of sports.

Blacken the boxes in row 3 that contain names of things that are *not* found in the sky.

Skip row 4. *Do not* blacken any boxes in row 4.

In row 5, blacken any boxes containing words that mean the same as "small."

In row 6, blacken any boxes containing words that mean the opposite of "cold."

In row 7, blacken any boxes containing words that rhyme with the word *game*.

Skip row 8.

Blacken the boxes in row 9 containing words that are names of vehicles or names of plants.

Blacken the boxes in row 10 containing the names of things that are round and can be eaten.

Blacken the boxes in row 11 containing the names of things that are *not* large and are *not* green.

Skip row 12.

In row 13, blacken any boxes containing words naming things that are small but are not animals.

In row 14, blacken any boxes containing words naming things that are green but are *not* things people eat.

In row 15, blacken any boxes containing words naming things that are *not* round and are *not* purple.

Now, turn the page sideways so that the star is at the top of the page. Find the word that is made by the boxes you blackened in. Write the word at the bottom of the page.

Answer Key

The hidden word is *ears*.

Additional Activities

1. Give a series of oral directions. Then, have students carry them out in the correct sequence. *(For example: Sharpen your pencil; name three U.S. presidents; close the door; recite the pledge to the flag; then sit down.)* Start with a short series of directions. Make it progressively more difficult.

2. Let students take turns giving a specified number of directions to other students in the class.

3. Give a series of directions involving school tasks. *(For example: Turn to page 219; find the third paragraph; say aloud the first word in the second sentence.)*

4. Orally, give directions to a certain location within the school. Have students listen to, then repeat or write down the directions.

Name _____   Date _____

LISTEN AND FOLLOW DIRECTIONS

Directions: You are going to hear a set of directions. Follow the directions to discover some equipment you can use to improve your listening skills. Use a pencil so you can erase if you need to.

	Volkswagen	Ford	Chevy	Jeep	Buick
1.	Volkswagen	Ford	Chevy	Jeep	Buick
2.	soccer	raking	skiing	mowing	tennis
3.	tree	cloud	rocket	star	roof
4.	moon	sun	oatmeal	small	clip
5.	tiny	little	wee	petite	mini
6.	cool	icy	warm	frozen	hot
7.	fame	shame	aim	blame	exclaim
8.	tame	car	name	airplane	bus
9.	truck	rose	daisy	violet	train
10.	tires	cookie	orange	bowl	doughnut
11.	mouse	iceberg	ant	tooth	raisin
12.	spider	egg	pen	ice	box
13.	needle	flea	penny	tack	seed
14.	grass	lettuce	leaf	celery	bush
15.	dog	tree	cat	earth	oatmeal

★

Write the word you discovered here: _____

10   *Following Directions*

FOLLOW A SERIES OF DIRECTIONS

Overview

In this exercise, students are required to follow a series of oral directions. This is a more difficult task because it requires concentrating for a longer period of time.

Instructions

Pass out copies of Exercise 4. Students should use a pencil when completing this exercise so they can erase any mistakes.

Read the following instructions aloud.

As you follow the directions I give, you will be making a drawing inside the box in Exercise 4. Listen carefully. Try not to miss any steps. If you do get behind, don't panic. You can pick up the directions at any point and keep going.

Let's begin. First, put your pencil on the capital letter *B* inside the box. Now connect the dots labeled with capital letters in this order: *B* to *X*, *X* to *Y*, *Y* to *O*, *O* to *L*, *L* to *R*, and *R* to *N*. (*Read these slowly, pausing between each pair of letters.*)

Next, find the small letter *b* and put your pencil on it. Now connect the dots labeled with small letters in this order: *b* to *y*, *y* to *o*, *o* to *d*, *d* to *r*, *r* to *n*, and *n* to *q*.

Find the large oval in the upper left corner of the drawing. Make three more large ovals like it in a column down the left side of the drawing.

Find the small oval in the upper right corner of the drawing. Make three more small ovals in a row across the top of the drawing.

Make four more large ovals in a row across the bottom of the drawing.

Make three more small ovals in a column down the right side of the drawing.

Make six more large ovals scattered through the middle of the drawing.

Make ten more small ovals scattered through the middle of the drawing.

Next, find the numbered lines at the bottom of the page.

On line 13, write the first letter in the word *mother*.

On line 10, write the letter that comes after *B* (as in boy) in the alphabet.

On line 5, write the letter that comes before *S* in the alphabet.

On line 3, write the letter that looks like a circle.

On line 9, write the first letter in the word *instructions*.

On line 4, write the letter *T*.

On line 11, write the letter that begins the word *job*.

On lines 6 and 12, write the letter that is the best letter grade you can get on a test.

On line 1, write the letter that comes after *T* in the alphabet.

On lines 2, 7, and 8, write the letter that begins the word *finished*.

This completes the instructions for Exercise 4. The words on the lines at the bottom of the page are the title of the drawing you made at the top of the page.

Answer Key

The title of the drawing is *UFO Traffic Jam*.

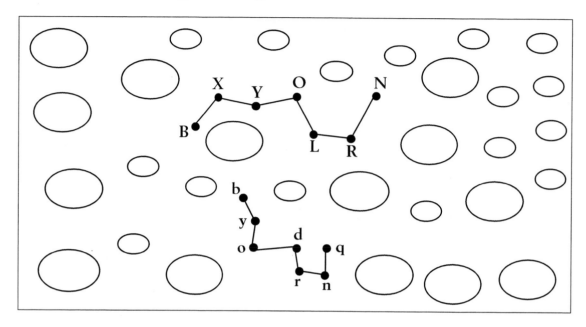

Additional Activities

1. Give students directions for drawing a scene. Then compare their drawings with one you have made ahead of time to see how well they have followed all the directions. (For example: Draw the sun in the upper right corner. Draw two trees on the left side of the drawing.)

2. Guide students in making various designs on paper by following your oral directions.

FOLLOW A SERIES OF DIRECTIONS

Directions: Follow the directions to complete this cartoon.

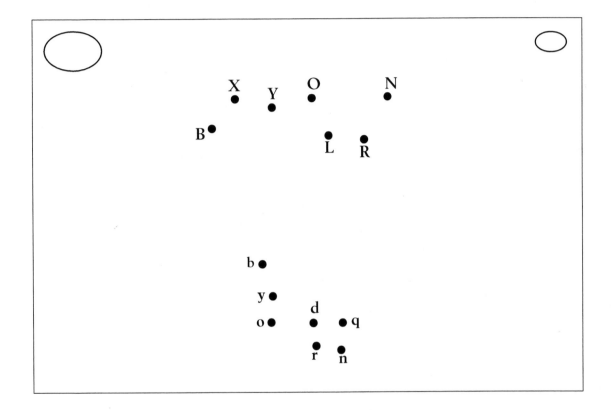

‾1‾ ‾2‾ ‾3‾   ‾4‾ ‾5‾ ‾6‾ ‾7‾ ‾8‾ ‾9‾ ‾10‾   ‾11‾ ‾12‾ ‾13‾

13   *Following Directions*

TAKE NOTES ON ASSIGNMENTS

Instructions

Discuss with the class the following tips for getting assignments right.

1. Have a special place to write down all assignments. A small notebook is a good way to do this.

2. Write assignments down. Don't trust your memory. You may think you'll remember. But hours later, you may find you've forgotten.

3. Pay full attention when assignments are given.

4. Ask questions if you don't understand.

Pass out copies of Exercise 5 to each student. Students are to take notes on the assignments in the boxes provided at the top of Exercise 5. Read the following aloud to the students. Read slowly, pausing to give students time to write.

English assignment: In your grammar workbook, do pages 9 and 10. These pages are on the usage of your (Y–O–U–R) and you're (Y–O–U–'–R–E). Then you are to review pages 1 through 10 in your grammar workbook for a test on Friday. Another thing: We need umbrellas for props in the class play. So, if you have one, please bring it to school. Last, the review session for the grammar test will be held after school, not before school as we had planned. So, if you need help, please stop in after school for the review session.

History assignment: Your reports on the Constitution are due on Wednesday. And, you are to learn Amendments 1 through 10 by Friday. For tomorrow, your notes on Chapter 7 are due. That should keep you busy!

Algebra assignment: Here is your assignment for tomorrow. You are to do the odd problems on page 478. Then on page 479, you only need to do every third problem. The subject of these two pages is division of fractions.

Vocabulary

assignment • notebook

Answer Key

1. Constitution
2. third
3. Wednesday
4. division
5. notes
6. review
7. learn
8. odd
9. umbrella
10. after
11. your, you're

The punch line to the joke is: *You could try anyway!*

Additional Activities

1. Give other oral assignments to the class. Have them practice writing down the assignments. Have students jot down only key words, not try to write the assignment word for word. For example, if the teacher says, "For Friday, do the odd problems on page 479," the student might write "Fri.: p. 479 odd probs."

2. Conduct practice sessions in which you give an assignment orally. Have students repeat it out loud, then write it down.

3. Be sure each student has a system for writing down all assignments. It could be a notebook or a section of a loose-leaf notebook.

4. Give small assignments throughout a class period. Students should write these down as they hear them. Give extra points for each assignment they have correctly written in their notes.

TAKE NOTES ON ASSIGNMENTS

Directions: As you listen, jot down your assignments in the space provided.

English	History	Algebra

Directions: Use the notes you made to answer these questions.

1. The history reports are to be on the _____ .

2. In algebra, you are to do every _____ problem on page 479.

3. The history reports are due on _____ . (Which day?)

4. The topic of the algebra assignment is _____ of fractions.

5. For history tomorrow, you are to hand in your _____ on Chapter 7.

6. _____ pages 1–10 in your grammar book for a test Friday.

7. _____ the first ten amendments to the Constitution by Friday.

8. In algebra, you are to do the _____ problems on page 478.

9. If possible, bring an _____ for a prop for the class play.

10. An extra review session for the grammar test will be _____ school tomorrow. (after, before)

11. The grammar assignment is on the correct usage of _____ and

_____ .

Directions: Write the first letter of each answer above on the blank with the same number. You will find the punch line to this joke.

Son: Dad, could you help me with this algebra assignment?
Dad: Well, I could, son, but it wouldn't be right, now, would it?
Son: I don't suppose so, but . . .

‾‾ ‾‾ ‾‾   ‾‾ ‾‾ ‾‾ ‾‾ ‾‾   ‾‾ ‾‾ ‾‾   ‾‾ ‾‾ ‾‾ ‾‾ ‾‾ ‾‾
11 8 9   1 8 9 7 4   2 6 11   10 5 11 3 10 11

Following Directions

DON'T MISS THE ASSIGNMENT

Overview

The purpose of Exercise 6 is to give students practice listening for directions given indirectly. On Exercise 6, students listen to four "mini-lectures." Embedded in each one is an assignment. Students are to listen for the assignment, then write it in the appropriate box on Exercise 6.

Instructions

Pass out copies of Exercise 6. Then, read the following information aloud to the class.

> Sometimes teachers give assignments in a very direct way. Other times, assignments may be given in the middle of a lecture or discussion. In order to get these assignments right, you must listen very carefully.
>
> The purpose of Exercise 6 is to give you practice getting assignments that are given indirectly. Look at Exercise 6. You will see that it is divided into five boxes. Find the box labeled Assignment 1. Listen as I read the first mini-lecture. When you hear the assignment, write it down in the box for Assignment 1. Here we go.
>
> **Assignment 1.** During the past 40 years, prices have gotten higher and higher. When prices keep going up, it's called *inflation*.
>
> Inflation can become a problem. This happens when people do not have enough dollars to buy what they need and want. They may have the same jobs and make the same money, but prices are higher. People can't buy what they did before.

> For example, a basket of food that cost $20 in 1990 cost about $30 in 2000. That's a big jump in just 10 years.
>
> When you go home tonight, I want you to talk to an older person, perhaps your parents. Find out how much it cost them to go out on a date when they were growing up. (For example, you could find out how much it cost them to go to a movie or out for a hamburger.) We'll list our findings on the board tomorrow and compare the costs of dates then and now.
>
> This is why inflation can be harmful. When prices double, the value of money is cut in half.

Did you get the assignment? You should have written it in the box for Assignment 1.

Let's go on to the next mini-lecture. Listen for the assignment. Write it in the box for Assignment 2. Let's begin.

> **Assignment 2.** The increase in knowledge about health and medicine over the past 100 years has been amazing.
>
> The first major step was Pasteur's discovery that germs cause disease. Then, Sir Joseph Lister revolutionized surgery by using antiseptics in 1865. The third major advance was the use of antibiotics against disease in the twentieth century.
>
> That reminds me, your reports on advances in health care will be due this Friday instead of Thursday. I will not accept any late papers.

Now then, let's see how these medical advances affect our lives. The average life expectancy for a person born in 1900 was 47.3 years. It had risen to 75 years for babies born in 1996. Why? Because we have a higher standard of living. Good food, clean homes, and better health care have also contributed to our longer lives.

Okay. You should have written Assignment 2 in the second box. Now let's move on to Assignment 3.

Assignment 3. We will be talking about electricity. The Greek philosopher Thales discovered static electricity almost 2,500 years ago. Since then, many people have experimented with electricity.

Thomas Edison invented the incandescent lamp, better known as the lightbulb, in 1879. Now America had a practical way to light homes and offices.

Tonight when you go home, I want you to look through your own homes and make a list of all the appliances and machines that operate on electricity.

Today's homes are electrical wonderlands. Electric power runs America today. It is often called "humanity's most useful servant."

I hope you have written Assignment 3 in the third box. We will now move on to Assignment 4.

Assignment 4. The subject of this mini-lecture is friction. Friction is a force that slows moving objects. A good tire produces friction between itself and the road. When the car is moving, there is little friction. But once the brakes are applied, the friction between the tires and the road stops the car quickly.

In some places we don't want friction. Wax on the bottom of snow skis reduces friction and makes them move faster over the snow. Oil and wax are lubricants that lessen friction between surfaces.

For tomorrow, I want you to think of one example in which friction is needed. Also, think of an example in which friction is not wanted. Write your examples down to hand in.

Remember, the more friction there is, the more force is needed to move an object. And the less friction there is, the less force needed to move the object.

We have made it to the last mini-lecture and the last box on Exercise 6. Let's get going!

Assignment 5. We will now talk about credit cards. A century ago, borrowing money was considered disgraceful. Certainly, a different attitude exists today! Most Americans carry one or more little plastic cards which allow them to charge hundreds or thousands of dollars worth of goods and services.

By the way, for Monday, I want you to find out what qualifications a person must have to get a credit card. You could look in the library, check the Internet, ask a bank officer, ask a store manager, or talk with your parents to find out how a person can get approved for a credit card. Write down what you find out and be ready to hand in your findings.

Although credit must be used wisely, it has played an important role in improving our living standard. Credit lets people buy anything—from a home to a vacation—and pay for it later. However, real money still has to enter the picture somewhere, as people try to pay off the bills they run up on those handy plastic cards.

This is the end of Exercise 6.

Instruct students to hand in their papers or get ready to check their work.

Answer Key

1. Assignment 1: For tomorrow, talk to an older person and find out how much a date used to cost when he or she was a teenager.

2. Assignment 2: Reports on advances in health care are due Friday.

3. Assignment 3: List the electrical things in your home.

4. Assignment 4: For tomorrow, write an example in which good friction is needed and one example in which friction is not wanted.

5. Assignment 5: For Monday, find out what qualifications you need to get a credit card.

Additional Activity

Give students additional practice by constructing more examples similar to those in Exercise 6.

DON'T MISS THE ASSIGNMENT

Directions: Listen to each mini-lecture. Within each lecture, you will be given an assignment. Write down each assignment in the correct box below.

Assignment 1: Inflation	Assignment 2: Health
Assignment 3: Electricity	**Assignment 4: Friction**
Assignment 5: Credit Cards	Q. How do you stop a charging herd of elephants? A. Take away their credit cards.

Following Directions

IDENTIFYING DIRECTION CUES

Instructions

Pass out copies of Exercise 7. (It is a two-page exercise.) Discuss how teachers make use of direction cues to guide students' attention to main ideas. Allow students to read the pages and answer the questions on their own.

Vocabulary

cue • alert • conclusion

Answer Key

1. Answers will vary.
2. Answers may vary. Suggested answer: You need to concentrate on what is being said. Read over the list of direction cues. Listen for those words or phrases.

Additional Activity

Allow students to work in pairs or small groups to make a list of direction cues used by some of their teachers.

EXERCISE 7

IDENTIFYING DIRECTION CUES

An alarm clock

A gong

A siren

A judge yelling "Order in the court!"

What do all these sounds have in common? Each is a way in which someone gets your attention.

Teachers also have ways of getting your attention. Usually, they are not as obvious as those just mentioned.

You can train your ears to catch the teacher's signals. You can learn what words a teacher uses to point out important points. These words are called **direction cues**.

Direction cues tell you to be alert: *Pay attention! The teacher is about to say something you should remember.* Here are some examples:

> Listen to what I am saying . . .
>
> Now, this is important . . .
>
> Because of this . . .
>
> Let us go over this point again . . .
>
> The result of this was . . .
>
> There are four main reasons . . .
>
> Don't forget . . .
>
> In summary . . .
>
> In conclusion . . .
>
> There are three . . . (four, two, ten, any number)

(continued)

IDENTIFYING DIRECTION CUES *(continued)*

Numbers can be important direction cues. For example, a teacher may say, "Today, we'll talk about the three main causes of the Civil War." Be sure you get all three points. If you end up with two in your notes, you'll know you're missing one.

Let's say you are in class listening to your teacher speak. You are taking notes on the material.

As the teacher talks, he or she will use direction cues. This is the signal for you to write down the idea that follows. It is an idea that the teacher wants you to remember. You will probably find it on a test later.

Train your ears to catch these direction cues. You'll find you have an easier time getting the main ideas of lectures or talks.

Finding Direction Cues

1. Make a list of some direction cues your teachers use when speaking in class.

   _____

   _____

   _____

   _____

   _____

   _____

2. How do you think you could train your ears to be more aware of a teacher's direction cues?

   _____

   _____

   _____

   _____

   _____

   _____

       Following Directions

GET THE DIRECTION CUES

Instructions

Pass out copies of Exercise 8 to each student. Slowly, read the lecture on Exercise 8 aloud as the students follow along. They are to underline the words that are direction cues as they hear them being read.

Answer Key

The following points should be underlined.

1. Paragraph 1: we're going to talk about . . .

2. Paragraph 2: The first important point is . . .

3. Paragraph 3: Let me point out that . . .

4. Paragraph 4: You must realize that . . .

5. Paragraph 5: the important point here is that . . .

6. Paragraph 6: remember that . . .

7. Paragraph 7: Don't forget that . . .

8. Paragraph 8: One term I want you to remember is . . .

9. Paragraph 9: whose name you should not forget . . . *and* you need to remember . . .

(The students' underlining need not exactly match what is printed here. They should underline approximately the same phrases, however.)

Additional Activity

Allow students to work in pairs. As the teacher speaks, they are to listen for direction cues. If one student hears a cue, he or she should alert the other. Students can make a list of direction cues heard. They should work quietly, so as not to interrupt the class.

Name _____   Date _____

GET THE DIRECTION CUES

Today, we're going to talk about the airplane as it was used in World War I.

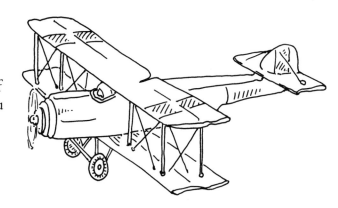

The first important point is that as World War I began, the airplane was not even thought of as a weapon. Generals of that time believed that to win battles you must have huge numbers of troops, artillery, and cavalry. There was no place in battle for planes.

Let me point out that as World War I began, airplanes were used mostly for scouting. Planes were used to observe troop movements. They located enemy artillery. They landed to pick up spies. An observer rode with each pilot. He outranked the pilot and gave all the orders.

You must realize that in the early days of the war, the pilots of the two sides were more like friends than enemies. Their planes were not armed. Often they waved at each other as they passed in the sky.

However, the important point here is that as the war continued, the pilots joined the fight. In early days, pilots threw half-bricks at each other. It soon proved almost impossible to hit anyone with them. So the pilots came up with the "bag of bricks" method. The idea was to fly over any enemy plane and drop the bag of bricks on its propeller. Few planes were ever downed with this fighting practice.

No one knows who fired the first shot from an airplane. Once again, remember that early attempts at shooting in the air were not successful. Flyers began to carry pistols in their planes. But no one ever shot down a plane with a pistol. Later, machine guns were used in planes. Some pilots fired through their own propellers and shot themselves down.

Don't forget that American pilots in World War I had no parachutes. The military couldn't make parachutes small enough to fit in a cockpit. The generals didn't like the idea of parachutes anyway. They said, "Pilots might jump out when they did not have to. We would lose too many planes that way."

One term I want you to remember is "the flying ace." An **ace** was a flyer who shot down more than five planes.

The most famous ace, whose name you should not forget, was the German flyer Baron von Richthofen, who shot down 80 planes. He was nicknamed the "Red Baron." Another ace you need to remember is Eddie Rickenbacker. He shot down 26 planes in less than 7 months.

USE DIRECTION CUES

Overview

Exercise 9 gives students more practice picking up direction cues.

Instructions

Pass out copies of Exercise 9. Explain that you will be reading aloud some information on the history of the automobile. As you talk, you will use six direction cues. The six cues you will use are listed in order in Exercise 9. Read through the six direction cues with the students. Instruct them to keep their eyes on Exercise 9. When students hear the first cue, they are to write down *the main idea that follows it* in their own words and in the space provided.

In might be a good idea to do direction cue 1 as a class. Remind students not to write the main idea word for word. They should write only key words, not complete sentences.

Read aloud the following information.

A wealthy man once wrote his funeral plans into his will. On the day of his funeral, he was placed behind the wheel of his luxury car. In a final attempt to "take it with him," the man and the machine were lowered slowly into the grave. As requested in the man's will, all of the luxury equipment was turned on. A stereo tape deck blared out music. A small color television glowed in the back seat. A small bar sat beside the television. A telephone rang constantly.

A young man passing by the cemetery stopped to watch the event. He looked at the leather upholstery and fine carpet that were visible. He watched all the luxury options in operation. Shaking his head in amazement, he said, "Man, now that's what I call living!"

As this joke shows, the automobile has been the subject of countless songs, jokes, movies, and stories. They have become symbols of wealth, status, and power. Cars today are much more than a material necessity. *The point I'm trying to make is* that cars often are a reflection of their owners' personalities.

For example, a solid, reliable Model T usually suggested the driver of the car was also solid and reliable. A flashy sports car was usually owned by a person who was trying to be flashy, too. Today, certain cars might be considered undignified for a doctor, mayor, or school principal to drive.

Around 1900, just owning a car was a symbol of prestige, because only the very rich could afford one. But as more people became able to afford cars, different types became available. The style of the car therefore began to be very important. At first, all cars were black. But soon, the color and style became as important as the engine.

Now, I want to point out six auto styles which have prevailed since World War II.

The first style of car I want you to remember was called the streamlined car. After World War II, cars were designed with flowing curves. These were supposed to be not only beautiful but also functional, as they caused less wind resistance.

A second car style you should remember was seen in the late 1950's. These jet-age cars had sharp lines and huge, sharklike fins. Some of the fins were so sharp they actually injured people who happened to touch them.

A third car style was the large car. In the early 1960's, the large car or limousine represented power, prestige, position, and wealth. Everyone who could drove big, flashy cars. President Lyndon Johnson had an entire fleet of luxury cars on his Texas ranch. Elvis Presley's love affair with the Cadillac was well known.

A fourth car style became popular during the gas shortages of the 1970's. At this time people wanted smaller, more fuel-efficient cars. The Volkswagen Beetle was the forerunner of the many smaller cars popular today.

The fifth and sixth styles, which are popular today, are the minivan and the sports utility vehicle. What will be next?

Answers

There will be some variation in how the main ideas are stated.

1. Cars show owners' personalities.
2. Six styles of cars since WWII
3. (1) Streamlined cars—flowing curves
4. (2) Late 1950's—fins, sharp lines
5. (3) Early 1960's—big cars, prestige
6. (4) 1970's—small cars, save gas
7. Today—(5) minivans, (6) sports utility vehicles

EXERCISE 9

USE DIRECTION CUES

Directions: Listen for these direction cues as read by your teacher. Write down the main idea that follows each direction cue.

Q. What is a history of cars called?
A. An **auto**biography.

1. The point I'm trying to make is . . .

2. Now, I want to point out six . . .

3. The first style of car I want you to remember . . .

4. A second car style you should remember . . .

5. A third car style was . . .

6. A fourth car style . . .

7. The fifth and sixth styles . . .

FOLLOW DIRECTION CUES

Instructions

Pass out copies of Exercise 10. Tell the class that you will be giving them a mini-lecture on the California Gold Rush. During this lecture, you will make five main points. You will use direction cues to emphasize the main points they are to remember.

Instruct students to listen for the direction cues. When they hear one, they should *write down the important point that follows it*. Remind students to write down these main ideas in their own words. They should write only key words, not complete sentences.

Tell students that you will give an assignment at the end of the mini-lecture. They are to write it down in the box labeled "Assignment."

If there are no questions, begin reading the information below. Read the direction cues, in italics, with some emphasis.

Today we will be talking about the California Gold Rush. *First of all, I want you to remember* that the Gold Rush began in 1849 at Sutter's Mill.

James Marshall was the first to find gold. At the time, he was building a mill on the California ranch of John Sutter. Marshall and Sutter tried to keep the gold a secret. But before long, the discovery was the best-known secret in the world. Within a year, there was a worldwide outbreak of "gold fever."

Just getting to California in 1849 was not easy. *You are to remember for the test* the three ways American gold seekers could choose to get to California: first, by wagon or horse on the overland routes;

second, by ship around South America; or third, by ship to Panama, then on foot across Panama, then onward by ship up the Pacific coast.

Gold seekers traveling overland got to California in all sorts of ways: not only by covered wagon, or what was called a prairie schooner, but also in horse-drawn carts, by horseback or muleback, by pushing wheelbarrows loaded with their worldly goods, and by just walking. They endured attacks by Native Americans, the scorching deserts, disease, hunger and thirst, and many other hardships.

Gold seekers traveling all the way by ship had to endure the stormy passage around Cape Horn. The weather was always terrible, and the passage often took 30 days to complete. The food was bad, consisting mainly of salted meat, fish, rice, beans, and hardtack. Seasickness was a major problem.

Wealthier gold seekers often chose the Panama route, but it was not easy either. Ships were so crowded that one New Yorker wrote: "The owners appeared to have taken the exact measurements of each man and filled the ship accordingly." Once they arrived in Panama, thousands died of cholera, malaria, and yellow fever in the jungles.

So, getting to California in 1849 was not easy. Now, *my third main point* is that once the gold seekers arrived in California, their life in the gold fields was very hard work. The work was lonely, and living conditions in the mining camps were terrible. Most of the would-be millionaires did not find any "pay dirt." In fact, most found it hard to even make a living. Many of the gold seekers died very young, unable to make a success of it.

One of the most important results of the Gold Rush was that the nearby village of San Francisco became a bustling city almost overnight. It was a city of violence, bad roads, and high prices for everything. When it rained, as it often did, the dirt streets became almost impossible to travel. Food was so expensive a small gold-find would soon be used up. It cost $2 for a loaf of bread, $6 for a pound of butter, $16 for a can of sardines, and $8 for a bottle of ale. (And that was in 1849!)

Now, *in conclusion, it is important to remember that* most of the gold seekers soon realized that the real wealth of California was not her gold but her soil and sunshine. Most of the gold seekers settled down to become farmers or merchants. But the Gold Rush had certainly speeded the development of California.

Don't forget that your reports on the California Gold Rush are due next Friday. Write a two-page report on any aspect of the Gold Rush that interests you. You might choose to discuss travel to California, a famous person of the Gold Rush, life in the mining camps, or any other part of the Gold Rush story that you find interesting.

Answers

Accept answers similar to these:

1. Gold Rush began—1849, Sutter's Mill
2. Three ways to get to California: overland, Cape Horn, Panama
3. Life hard in gold fields
4. Gold Rush made San Francisco a city
5. Many gold seekers became farmers, merchants

Assignment: 2-page report on Gold Rush, Friday

EXERCISE 10

FOLLOW DIRECTION CUES

Directions: As you listen to your teacher, write the five main points from the talk on the California Gold Rush here. Also, write the assignment given by your teacher at the end of the talk.

Main Point 1:	Main Point 2:
Main Point 3:	**Main Point 4:**
Main Point 5:	**Assignment:**

YOU CAN GET THERE FROM HERE!

Instructions

Pass out copies of Exercise 11. Tell students that the purpose of Exercise 11 is for them to apply their listening skills to follow directions to find a location.

Point out the compass on the map in Exercise 11. Make sure that students understand the directions—north, south, east, and west—on the map.

Read aloud the following information slowly and carefully.

> You are taking a trip. You are in an unfamiliar area when the need to get to a hospital suddenly arises. You stop and get directions from a local person.
>
> Listen carefully to the directions. As you hear them, mark that route on the map in Exercise 11. When you have finished, put an X on the building you think is the hospital.
>
> Let's begin.
>
> First, locate your car. It is in the bottom left corner on the map. You have stopped your car on the shoulder of the road, where you have just asked directions to the hospital.
>
> Follow the directions given to you by Joe Local:
>
> First, get back on the Interstate 55 (I-55) going north.
>
> Second, take the second exit and turn right.
>
> When you get to the Extra Gas Station, go north.
>
> Drive past the college campus, and then take the first right.
>
> Go straight until you come to the next intersection.
>
> Then, turn left and follow the road as it curves around and heads south.
>
> Go straight for about two blocks.
>
> Then, head west on the road that goes around Jackson Pond.
>
> Then, take the first left.
>
> Turn left again at the next intersection.
>
> The hospital is the second building you come to on the north side of the road. Mark a large X on the building you think is the hospital.

Instruct students to answer the two questions at the bottom of Exercise 11. In these questions, students need to give directions to two different places found on the map. They should give the shortest, most direct route possible.

Answer Key

The hospital is the building on the right directly south of Jackson Pond.

For questions 1 and 2, accept directions that are similar to the ones below. Do not accept less direct routes.

1. Go one-half block west to the corner. Turn left and go two blocks south. Turn right. You'll see the motel on your left.
2. Go one and one-half blocks east. Turn left and go one and one-half blocks north. The shopping center is on your right.

Additional Activities

1. Obtain simple maps, or make one yourself and photocopy it. (You can even try a map of your school.) Without revealing the destinations, give directions to various places. See if students arrive at the correct spots.

2. Divide the class into pairs. Have students practice giving oral directions to particular places on their maps.

3. Have each person in the class choose a location in the school. Then, he or she should give directions to that spot aloud to the class, without revealing the chosen destination. See whether class members can follow the directions and identify the destination.

EXERCISE 11

YOU CAN GET THERE FROM HERE!

Directions: Follow the directions your teacher reads to locate the hospital. Mark an X on the hospital.

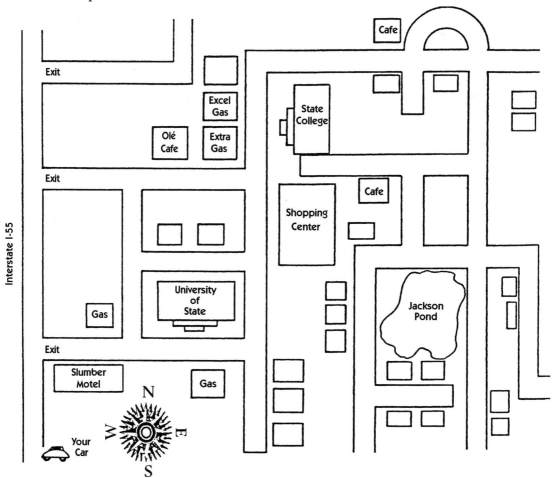

1. Give directions for how to get from the Olé Cafe to the Slumber Motel. Take the most direct route.

2. Give directions for how to get from the Slumber Motel to the Shopping Center. Take the most direct route.

DELIVER THE MONEY

Instructions

Discuss with the class the importance of following directions accurately on the job. Point out that keeping a job may depend partly on the ability to follow directions.

Pass out copies of Exercise 12 to the class. Explain to students that in this exercise, they have been hired as delivery people for Sampson's Armored Car Service. The job is to pick up and deliver various amounts of money to different businesses in town. It is important that deliveries be made accurately, as sometimes large amounts of money are involved.

Read the following instructions aloud to the students.

Exercise 12 is a work order for your job as a delivery person. Look at Exercise 12. Just above the chart, you see the words, "Delivery Schedule for: (blank)." On the blank, write your name.

Write today's date on the line labeled "Date."

Below the date, you see four boldfaced words in columns. The first column is headed "Time." In this column, write the time when you should deliver the money to the customer.

The second column is headed "Business Name and Address." In this column, write the name of the business where you need to deliver the money. If you are given the address of the company, write it here too.

In the third column, labeled "Amount of Money," write how much money is to be delivered.

Finally, the fourth column is headed "Special Instructions." Here you have room to put other instructions you are given regarding that delivery. Some examples of instructions that would go in this space could be: "Enter by the rear door" or "No bills larger than $10" or "Our parking lot is on Main Street" and so on.

Now you are ready to complete the work order. Your first delivery has been written on the work order as an example, so you can just follow along as I read.

Let's begin. Remember, the first stop is an example. Your first stop is to be made at 8:00. You will deliver $20,000 to the Ticonderoga Oil Company. The address is 1511 Northside Drive. Deliver the money only to Mr. O. I. Ell in person.

Now get ready to write down the rest of your deliveries.

Your second stop should be made at 8:30. It will be at the Big Sky Company. Their address is 123 Main Street. You will be delivering $1,000. You are to go in the side door and ask for Mr. Rivera.

Third, you'll go to the Star Grocery on Main Street. Be there by 9:00. You will deliver $5,000. Give the money to Mr. Johnson.

Your fourth stop should be made at 9:30. You will go to the City Bank on Pearl Street. You will deliver $50,000. Your contact person is Ms. Walden.

Your fifth delivery is to be made at 10:30. It will be to the Z-Mart. You will deliver $15,000. Go to the north entrance of the store. Wait for Mr. Li to meet you.

Finally, your sixth stop will be at the Tasty Donut Shop. This stop can be made any time before noon. You will deliver $500. While you are there, pick up two dozen

chocolate donuts for the employees' meeting I'm holding this afternoon.

Good luck with your deliveries!

Answer Key

Time	Business Name and Address	Amount of Money	Special Instructions
8:30	Big Sky Co. 123 Main St.	$1,000	Go in side door. Ask for Mr. Rivera.
9:00	Star Grocery on Main St.	$5,000	Give money to Mr. Johnson.
9:30	City Bank on Pearl St.	$50,000	Contact person is Ms. Walden.
10:30	Z-Mart	$15,000	Wait for Mr. Li at north entrance.
Before noon	Tasty Donut Shop	$500	Pick up two dozen chocolate donuts.

Additional Activities

1. Have students practice taking messages that are given to them "over the phone," as one might do in many job situations.

2. Orally give students a list of items to be bought at the store. See how many they can repeat aloud or write down correctly.

Name _____ Date _____

DELIVER THE MONEY

Sampson's Armored Car Service
Work Order

Delivery Schedule for: _____

Date: _____

	Time	Business Name and Address	Amount of Money	Special Instructions
1.	8:00	Ticonderoga Oil Co. 1511 Northside Dr.	$20,000	Give money only to Mr. O. I. Ell in person.
2.				
3.				
4.				
5.				
6.				

SOLVE THE CRIME

Instructions

Pass out copies of Exercise 13 to the class. Read aloud the following information.

> In Exercise 13, you will play the part of a detective trying to solve a robbery case. The victim is Mr. Wilson, owner of the Quickie Convenience Store. For the next few minutes, you will hear the chief of detectives interviewing Mr. Wilson and three witnesses to the crime.
>
> As a detective, you are expected to listen carefully and take notes on the important facts in the case which your chief will point out. Write your notes in the boxes provided at the top of Exercise 13.
>
> Look at Exercise 13. You will see that there is space provided for notes on the robber's description, the getaway car's description, and other important facts. For now, don't worry about the information at the bottom of the page. Listen as the chief of detectives conducts the interviews. In the boxes provided, take notes on the important points of the interview.
>
> Let's begin. This is the chief of detectives speaking.
>
> > **Chief:** Now detectives, you must first note that at 2:00 A.M. Tuesday, Mr. Wilson was robbed of $417 in cash. Please make a note of that time and amount.
> >
> > Now, we will interview Mr. Wilson. Mr. Wilson, what can you tell us about the robbery?

Mr. Wilson: Well, it was about 2:00 in the morning. The Quickie was nearly empty; there was only one customer buying some coffee. I was reading my horoscope in the *National Enquirer* when a man came in the back door from the storeroom. He came up behind me and grabbed me and tied me up.

He was about 5 feet, 5 inches tall. He wore blue jeans and a blue work shirt. He had a black ski mask over his head. He was on the heavy side, maybe 175 pounds. Well, come to think of it, I guess I'm not really sure it was a man; it might have been a woman.

After he took my money, he ran out of the store and jumped into a car. I think it was black. It might have been blue. Anyway, it was a newer car, one of those sports cars, maybe a Camaro or a Trans Am.

Chief: The next witness is Miss Mendez. She was in the store at the time of the robbery. Let's listen to what she saw.

Miss Mendez: I had just gotten off work at the City Hospital. I had stopped for a cup of coffee and a doughnut on my way home. This person came in wearing a blue work shirt, blue jeans, and a black ski mask. He was about 5 feet, 6 inches tall and sort of fat. He had blue eyes. Afterward, he drove away real fast in a bright blue Trans Am or Camaro, I'm not sure which.

Chief: Two questions, Miss Mendez. Are you sure it was a man? And are you sure the car was bright blue?

Miss Mendez: Oh yes. I just love that color of blue. My little car is painted the same blue. But, I guess it could have been a woman. I never thought of it.

Chief: Okay. Let's hear our final witness. Mr. Logan was stopped at the traffic light outside the store when the suspect ran a red light. Tell us what you saw, Mr. Logan.

Mr. Logan: I was stopped at the red light when this blue Trans Am came 90 miles an hour out of the parking lot by the convenience store. It ran right through a red light. I didn't get the license plate; it was too dark. I couldn't see inside the car.

Chief: Thank you all very much for your help. Now, let's put the facts together to solve the crime. If you took good notes, you'll be able to identify the right culprit.

Look at Exercise 13. At the bottom of the page, there are descriptions of four suspects who are being questioned by the police. Decide which suspect most closely matches the description of the robber given by the witnesses. Underline every part of each description that does not fit the clues you were given. Circle the name of the suspect you feel most likely committed the crime.

Answer Key

1. Suspect 1 is too tall and owns the wrong car.
2. Suspect 2 was seen at Smith's Bar & Grill at 2:00 A.M.
3. Suspect 3 most likely committed the crime.
4. Suspect 4 is too thin, has the wrong eye color, and owns the wrong car.

EXERCISE 13

SOLVE THE CRIME

Directions: Listen carefully to the interviews read by your teacher. In the boxes below, write your notes on the important facts in the case.

Time of robbery:	
What was stolen:	
Description of robber:	Description of car:

Suspects

Suspect No. 1: Big Red Smith
Height: 6'2"
Weight: 175 pounds
Shoulder-length brown hair; blue eyes
Previously convicted of robbery
Owns 3-year-old blue Camaro
Alibi: At home watching *Star Trek* reruns
(unconfirmed by witnesses)

Suspect No. 3: Light-fingered Lefty
Height: 5'6"
Weight: 182 pounds
Red hair, blue eyes
No previous record
Owns 1-year-old blue Trans Am
Alibi: At the movies (no witnesses)

Suspect No. 2: Shifty Sheila
Height: 5'4"
Weight: 170 pounds
Long blond hair, blue eyes
No previous record
Owns new blue Trans Am
Alibi: At Smith's Bar & Grill at 2:00 A.M.
(two witnesses)

Suspect No. 4: Testy Theresa
Height: 5'7"
Weight: 135 pounds
Blond hair, green eyes
Previous shoplifting conviction
Owns new black Trans Am
Alibi: At all-night grocery store doing her
shopping (no witnesses)

Part Two

Following Written Directions

14: DIRECTION VOCABULARY I
15: DIRECTION VOCABULARY II
16: DIRECTION VOCABULARY III

Overview

The purpose of Exercises 14–16 is to review vocabulary commonly found in written directions.

Instructions

Read the list of vocabulary and definitions found at the top of each page. Discuss any words that students find difficult. Some of the words are very basic—for example, *circle* and *underline*. These words are found in Direction Vocabulary I. The words in Direction Vocabulary II and III are more difficult. Be sure students understand the meaning of each word before you proceed.

Answer Key

Exercise 14: Direction Vocabulary I

Students should not answer questions 2 or 3.

Other answers will vary. Check papers to see that directions were followed.

Exercise 15: Direction Vocabulary II

1. outline
2. sequence
3. summarize
4. antonym
5. synonym
6. similar
7. prove
8. classify
9. compare
10. discuss

Exercise 16: Direction Vocabulary III

1. Tell the route the journey took from one point to the next.

2. Give reasons they would use to make building in the floodplain seem reasonable.

3. List reasons you chose plumbing.

4. Give strong and weak points about what you've learned.

5. Give examples of centrifugal force at work.

6. Break the causes into smaller parts and take a close look at each.

7. Tell how they are different.

8. Give the good and bad points of the character.

9. Give the main points about the effects of welfare.

Additional Activities

1. Have students write each vocabulary word (from the three exercises) in sentences.

2. Construct more examples of instructions using these words.

3. Have students write instructions using the vocabulary words. Let them take turns presenting these to the class. Other students can tell what the instructions mean.

4. Have students bring examples of the vocabulary as it is used in test instructions from classes they are taking. Discuss the meaning of the instructions.

DIRECTION VOCABULARY 1

Directions: Read the direction vocabulary words carefully. Be sure you understand what each word means. Then read and follow the directions below.

Direction Vocabulary Words

column	words or numbers in a vertical line	**name**	identify by name
define	give the meaning	**print**	writing like this: Print
describe	tell about in detail	**row**	a line of words or numbers printed across the page
explain	make plain or clear	**write**	use script like this: *Write*
item	one question or sentence on a test	**circle**	put a line around
list	write down one by one	**underline**	draw a line under

1. Read through items 1–4 before you start to work.

2. Circle the letter "e" every time you see it on this page.

3. Write the names of 10 animals smaller than a mouse here:

4. Do not answer questions 2 or 3. If you answered items 2 or 3, you have (*circle one choice*):

    (a) followed the directions   (b) not followed the directions.

    Go on to question 5.

5. Write the names of three classmates in a column in the right margin of this page.

6. List any three United States presidents in a row here:

7. Print your full name on the line:

_____   _____   _____
    Last   *First*   *Middle*

(continued)

DIRECTION VOCABULARY I *(continued)*

8. Describe, in 10 words or less, what you think a flying saucer looks like.

9. Explain why following directions is important on the job.

10. Define the word *instructions*.

11. In each row, look at the first word. Then underline any other word(s) in that row that exactly matches the first word.

    ROW 1:   define   describe   define   define   definite

    ROW 2:   describe   define   describe   description   desert

    ROW 3:   column   collect   column   Columbus   column

EXERCISE 15

DIRECTION VOCABULARY II

Directions: Read the direction vocabulary words carefully. Be sure you understand what each word means. Then use the words to fill in the blanks below. Use each word only once.

Direction Vocabulary Words			
antonym	a word that means the opposite of another word	**prove**	give proof of
		sequence	in correct order
classify	organize into categories	**similar**	almost the same, but not identical
compare	tell how two things are the same and/or different	**summarize**	give the main idea
discuss	talk or write about a subject	**synonym**	a word that means the same as another word
outline	give the main points		

Sample Test: Great Mysteries of Our Time

1. Here is an example of an _____: I. Three Modern Monsters
   (a) Big Foot
   (b) Loch Ness Monster
   (c) ghosts and witches

2. Put the events below into correct time _____ by numbering each one 1, 2, or 3:
   King Tut's tomb was discovered in 1923.
   Twenty-three researchers who examined Tut's treasures died mysteriously.
   King Tut reigned in Egypt.

3. S _____ your views on the Bermuda Triangle Mystery in one paragraph.

4. *Fact* is an _____ for *fiction*.

(continued)

EXERCISE 15

DIRECTION VOCABULARY II *(continued)*

5. *Mystery* is an _____ for *puzzle*.

6. *Astronomy* is a word that looks _____ to and is sometimes confused with the word *astrology*.

7. How did scientists _____ that the Cardiff giant (supposedly a 10-foot-tall petrified caveman) was a fraud?

8. _____ the subjects below into two groups: those you believe in and those you do not.

UFO's	witches	reading one's
Big Foot	astrology	fortune in tea
ESP	handwriting	leaves
ghosts	analysis	a crystal ball

9. _____ crystal ball gazing with telling one's fortune by palm reading. How are they alike? How are they different?

10. _____ your views on Big Foot. Do you believe it exists?

EXERCISE 16

DIRECTION VOCABULARY III

Directions: Read the direction vocabulary words carefully. Be sure you understand what each word means. Then read and follow the directions below.

Direction Vocabulary Words			
analyze	to break into parts and study	justify	prove to be just, right, or true
contrast	tell the differences	illustrate	give examples and explain
criticize	judge the good and bad points of		them
enumerate	list; name one by one	review	look over or study again
evaluate	look at and tell the worth of	trace	follow the course or trail of

Explain what each test question below asks you to do. (Don't answer the question itself.)

1. Trace the path of the Lewis and Clark expedition. _____
   _____

2. Tell how developers might justify building in a flood plain. _____
   _____

3. Enumerate your reasons for choosing plumbing as a trade. _____
   _____

4. Evaluate what you've learned in Spanish class this year. _____
   _____

5. Illustrate the principle of centrifugal force. _____
   _____

6. Analyze the causes of the Titanic disaster. _____
   _____

7. Contrast fish and sharks. _____
   _____

8. Criticize the main character in *The Scarlet Letter.* _____
   _____

9. Review the impact of welfare on modern society. _____
   _____

TEACHER PAGE

17: MULTIPLE-STEP INSTRUCTIONS
18: WHO FOLLOWED THE INSTRUCTIONS?

Overview

These exercises give students practice in analyzing multiple-step instructions. They teach students how to break the instructions into small steps that can be easily followed.

Instructions

Go over the instructions on the top of Exercise 17 with the class. Be sure everyone knows what to do. Allow students to complete both exercises on their own.

Answer Key

Exercise 17: Multiple-Step Instructions

Sample Assignment 1

1. The purpose of the assignment is to learn new vocabulary words each week.
2. There are four steps in the assignment.
3. Put a checkmark by: *Define the words; Write sentences; Study the words;* and *Copy the words.*

Sample Assignment 2

1. The directions tell you how to paint correctly.
2. There are six steps in the directions.
3. Put a check by: *Patch holes and cracks* and *Start at the top and paint your way down.*

Exercise 18: Who Followed the Instructions?

1. *Instructions 1:* 1. No 2. No 3. No 4. Yes 5. No
2. *Instructions 2:* 1. No 2. No 3. No 4. Yes 5. Yes

Additional Activities

1. Have students bring in additional sets of directions. These could come from a variety of sources: teacher directions, product labels, instructions for filling out forms, etc. Have students work in pairs to analyze the directions according to the method they have been given.
2. See the additional activities listed under Exercises 29–33 for ideas on more practice material you could use.

Name _____ Date _____

MULTIPLE-STEP INSTRUCTIONS

Often directions have several steps. If so, do these things when you read the directions.

 1. Read through all the directions.
 2. Number the steps you are to follow.
 3. Do each step one at a time.
 4. Read the directions to check your work.

Directions: In the two boxes that follow, you will find sample multiple-step instructions. Read the instructions. Then, answer the questions below the instructions.

> Each week I will give you a list of 20 vocabulary words. You are to write down each word in your vocabulary notebook. Then, give the definition of the word. Also write each word in a sentence. Study that week's list and know the definitions for a test we'll have each Friday.

 1. Read through all the directions. What is the purpose of this assignment?

 2. Number the steps you are asked to do. There are _____ steps in this assignment.

 3. Check off each step that you were asked to do.

    _____ Say each word out loud.   _____ Study the words.

    _____ Define the words.   _____ Alphabetize the words.

    _____ Write sentences.   _____ Copy the words.

 4. Read the directions again and check your answers.

(continued)

Name _____ Date _____

EXERCISE 17

MULTIPLE-STEP INSTRUCTIONS *(continued)*

Clean the walls with some cleanser and warm water. Then, patch any holes or cracks. As you paint, dip your paintbrush only one-third of its length into the paint. (Never put too much paint on your brush or it will drip all over!) Tap the brush lightly to get rid of the extra paint. Use light, long strokes as you brush the paint onto the wall. Start at the top of the wall and work your way down.

1. Read through all the directions. What is the purpose of these directions?

2. Number the steps you are asked to do. There are _____ steps in these directions.

3. Check off each step that you were asked to do.

_____ Put lots of paint on your brush.   _____ Patch holes and cracks.

_____ Wipe the brush on the can rim.   _____ Paint with short strokes.

_____ Dip the brush into the paint up   _____ Start at the top and paint
        to the brush handle.   your way down.

4. Read the directions again and check your answers.

EXERCISE 18

WHO FOLLOWED THE INSTRUCTIONS?

Directions: Read the boxed instructions below. Number the things you are asked to do. (Hint: The first set of instructions asks you to do six things. The second set has eight steps.) Then read what some people did after reading the instructions. If the person followed the instructions, write *Yes* on the line. If not, write *No* on the line.

Job Applicants

Arrive at the Courthouse between 8:30 and 8:45 A.M. on Tuesday, January 3. Go to Room 209 on the second floor. Pick up your examination paper there. Then go to Room 213 to take the examination. You must bring two No. 2 pencils and your identification. No one may enter the room after 9:00, when the exam will start.

_____ 1. Carol went to Room 213 to pick up her exam.

_____ 2. Dorothy wrote her exam in black pen.

_____ 3. Allen went to Room 209 at 9:00 to take his exam.

_____ 4. Sasha arrived at the Courthouse at 8:30 on January 3.

_____ 5. George was running late, so he went directly to Room 213 to take the exam at 9:00.

In Case of Accident

Don't leave the scene of the accident. Call the police. Call an ambulance if anyone is hurt. Give the other driver your name, address, phone number, driver's license number, car license number, registration number, and insurance company's name. Get the same information from the other driver. Get the names, addresses, and phone numbers of any witnesses. Do not admit you are at fault, even if you think you are. Call your insurance company immediately.

_____ 1. Carlos went directly home to phone the police and the insurance company after his accident.

_____ 2. Joey apologized to the other driver for causing the accident.

_____ 3. Sue would only give the other driver her name and phone number.

_____ 4. Mark got the names, addresses, and phone numbers of two witnesses to the accident.

_____ 5. Maria called the police, an ambulance, and her insurance company from a pay telephone on the corner where the accident occurred.

19: GENERAL TEST-TAKING DIRECTIONS
20: UNDERSTANDING INSTRUCTIONS ON TESTS
21: MULTIPLE-CHOICE QUESTIONS
22: MULTIPLE-CHOICE TEST DIRECTIONS
23: TRUE-FALSE QUESTION DIRECTIONS
24: MATCHING AND FILL-IN QUESTION DIRECTIONS
25: FIND THE MISTAKES
26: WRITING TEST QUESTIONS
27: USING A STANDARDIZED ANSWER SHEET

Overview

The purpose of this group of exercises is to make students aware of the importance of following directions carefully on tests. Simply reading instructions and following them exactly can improve student test scores. Directions commonly used on a variety of types of objective and essay tests are discussed in these exercises.

Answer Key

Exercise 19: General Test-Taking Directions

Put an X by: 2, 3, 4, 5, 6

Exercise 20: Understanding Instructions on Tests

Answers will vary. Suggested answers are:

1. 20 minutes for each question
2. 20 minutes on the 40-point question and about 7 minutes each on the 4 shorter questions
3. About a minute for each multiple-choice question and 20 minutes for the essay.
4. Plan your time so you don't spend too much time on any one question and run out of time to finish and review the test.

Exercise 21: Multiple-Choice Questions

1. Circle the letter of the *best* answer. (There may be more than one answer that is correct or partially correct.)
2. Write the letter of the answer on the line. (Don't circle it.)
3. Don't write on the test. Use the answer sheet.
4. Circle the incorrect answer.
5. Circle the letters of all correct answers. (There may be more than one.)
6. Underline the wrong answer and tell why it is wrong.
7. Circle a word that is *not* correct.

Exercise 22: Multiple-Choice Test Directions

1. d
2. a, b, d
3. a, b, c
4. a
5. c
6. b
7. a, b, c

```
a  ( 1   6   t   h   p   r   e   s   i   d   e   n   t )  o   p
( a ) b   v   c   b   g   u   t   i   j   h   g   t   e   t  ( l )
  t   i   r ( e   t   a   r   t   n   e   c   n   o   c ) l   i
  h   j   d   e ( h ) d   c   v   g   t   f   e   r   k   l   s
  o   d   c   a ( i ) d ( m   u   s   i   c ) d   r   t   y   t
  m   e   a   l ( n ) d   f   g   r   t   y   u   r ( r ) o   e
  e   l   e   p ( k ) d   c   v   b   g   u   j   g ( a ) r   n
  o ( a   t   s   c   h   o   o   l ) d   f   e   s   e   l   e
  b   c   d   e   r   t   u   h   g   e   d   a   b   b   a ( a )
( r   e   c   t   a   n   g   l   e ) e   d   f   r   y   e   t
  u ( s ) d   f   g   c   e   x   a   z   w   s   e   l   o   w
  i ( r ) i   e ( t   i   r   e   s ) p   o   e   r   z   o   o
  l ( o ) d   f   g ( g   i   r   a   f   f   e ) o   z   u   r
  o ( h ) d   c   v   g   f   b   t   g   y   h   e   i   i   k
  d   f   g   v   c   b   v   e   d   f   k   l   e   r   k   j
  o ( s   u   p   e   r   m   a   n ) d   f   r   t ( g ) l   i
```

Exercise 23: True-False Question Directions

1. False	6. False
2. False	7. False
3. True	8. False
4. False	9. False
5. True	10. True

Exercise 24: Matching and Fill-in Question Directions

true-false	b
fill-in	c
essay	d
multiple-choice	a
matching	e

1. short   2. sentences   3. words

Exercise 25: Find the Mistakes

1. name in wrong order; no middle name given
2. no date
3. no teacher's name
4. Section I: wrote *true/false* instead of + and 0
5. Section II: answer *b* should be used twice (on test directions and medicine)
6. Section III: wrote two sentences
7. Section IV: wrote 10 words
8. Section V: wrote *Correct* and *Incorrect* instead of C and *I*

9. Section VI: underlined answer instead of circling correct answer

Exercise 26: Writing Test Questions

Answers will vary.

Exercise 27: Using a Standardized Answer Sheet

1. There is a stray mark on answer *B*.

2. Answer *D* is crossed out rather than erased.

3. Both *B* and *E* are marked.

4. The area between two answers is shaded in.

5. Correct

6. d

7. c

8. b

9. d

10. a

Additional Activities

1. Collect various oral and written tests on which students can practice following directions. Test content should be kept easy and directions more difficult, as the purpose of the exercise is to follow directions, not test subject matter.

2. In your classroom assignments, give extra points for following directions exactly.

Name _____   Date _____

GENERAL TEST-TAKING DIRECTIONS

Directions: Read the boxed directions for improving your test-taking skills. Then put an *X* by each person below who used good test-taking skills.

Taking a Test

- Look over the whole test. Find out how long it is. See what kinds of questions are asked.
- Plan your time. Don't spend too much time on any one section, unless it is worth a lot of points.
- If you don't know an answer, you have two choices:
- Skip it and come back to it when you've finished the rest of the test.
- Guess (if points aren't subtracted for wrong answers).
- Listen to the teacher's instructions before the test starts.
- Follow all directions carefully. Look for direction cues (*see Exercises 15 and 16*). Do exactly what the questions ask for.
- Check your work. Change your answer only if you are sure it's wrong. First answers are often the best.

---

1. _____ Eric didn't want to waste time. He started filling out his test as the teacher gave instructions.

2. _____ Joyce skipped every question she didn't know. Later, she came back to them and tried to think them through.

3. _____ Eli looked over the whole test before he began.

4. _____ Mark saw that one question was worth 50 points (out of 100). He planned to spend about half of his time on that question.

5. _____ The directions on the science test said to list five advances in modern medicine. Cheryl made a list, numbering her points from 1 to 5.

6. _____ Reggie read over his test after he'd finished. He was unsure about three of his answers. So, he left them the way he had first answered them.

7. _____ Marti didn't understand why her teacher had said it was OK to guess on some answers. She decided it was smarter to leave those blank rather than pick a wrong answer.

Name _____   Date _____

UNDERSTANDING INSTRUCTIONS ON TESTS

There are two main kinds of test questions.

1. **Essay questions** ask you to write a paragraph (or more) to answer a question. In your answer, you give a main idea and examples to support it.

2. **Objective questions** ask for short, factual answers. Objective questions include: multiple-choice, matching, true-false, and fill-in questions.

You can score higher on all kinds of tests by carefully following the directions given. Also, there are tricks that will make answering these questions easier.

Let's look first at ways to improve your score on essay questions. Then, in Exercises 21–24, you'll find hints for objective questions.

Essay Questions

1. Look over the test briefly. See how many questions there are and which may require the most time. If there are three essay questions on the test, all worth the same number of points, you might divide your time equally among them. Check the clock occasionally to make sure you're not running out of time.

2. Read each question carefully. Look for direction cues that tell what the teacher is looking for in an answer. Many of these direction cues are defined in Exercises 14–16.

Directions: Tell how you might plan your time when taking each of the following tests.

1. You have 60 minutes. The test has 3 essay questions, each worth 33 points.

2. You have 50 minutes. The test has 1 essay question worth 40 points and 4 short-answer essay questions worth 15 points each.

3. You have 45 minutes. There are 20 multiple-choice questions (each worth 3 points) and 1 essay question worth 40 points.

4. Why do you think it's a good idea to plan your time when taking a test?

EXERCISE 21

MULTIPLE-CHOICE QUESTIONS

Objective tests often include multiple-choice questions. These questions include four or five possible answers. Usually, the directions go something like this:

Read each sentence. Circle the letter of the correct answer.

There's no problem with these directions. The problem comes when students assume that **all** multiple-choice questions will have these same directions. **There are many possible variations on the basic directions.** So, pay attention. Why lose points for not reading directions?

Directions: Read each set of instructions below. Tell how the instructions are different from those given at the top of the page.

1. Read each sentence. Circle the letter of the best answer.

2. Read each sentence. Write the letter of the correct answer on the line in front of the sentence.

3. Read each sentence. Write the letter of the correct answer on the answer sheet provided. DO NOT write on this test.

4. Read each sentence. Three answers are correct. One answer is incorrect. Circle the letter of the incorrect answer.

5. Read each sentence below. One or more of the answers that follow it are correct. Circle the letter of each correct answer or answers.

6. Read each sentence below. Underline the answer that is incorrect. Write one sentence telling why it is incorrect.

7. Circle the word which is not a characteristic of fish.

MULTIPLE-CHOICE TEST DIRECTIONS

Directions: Read each set of numbered directions on page 59 **carefully** before answering the question. Underline each correct answer. Be sure to follow the directions exactly. Then, find and circle in the puzzle the thirteen answers you underlined. Words may go up, down, backward, or forward. (Only the correctly underlined answers will appear in the puzzle.) An example has been done for you.

a	1	6	t	h	p	r	e	s	i	d	e	n	t	o	p
a	b	v	c	b	g	u	t	i	j	h	g	t	e	t	l
t	i	r	e	t	a	r	t	n	e	c	n	o	c	l	i
h	j	d	e	h	d	c	v	g	t	f	e	r	k	l	s
o	d	c	a	i	d	m	u	s	i	c	d	r	t	y	t
m	e	a	l	n	d	f	g	r	t	y	u	r	r	o	e
e	l	e	p	k	d	c	v	b	g	u	j	g	a	r	n
o	a	t	s	c	h	o	o	l	d	f	e	s	e	l	e
b	c	d	e	r	t	u	h	g	e	d	a	b	b	a	a
r	e	c	t	a	n	g	l	e	e	d	f	r	y	e	t
u	s	d	f	g	c	e	x	a	z	w	s	e	l	o	w
i	r	i	e	t	i	r	e	s	p	o	e	r	z	o	o
l	o	d	f	g	g	i	r	a	f	f	e	o	z	u	r
o	h	d	c	v	g	f	b	t	g	y	h	e	i	i	k
d	f	g	v	c	b	v	e	d	f	k	l	e	r	k	j
o	s	u	p	e	r	m	a	n	d	f	r	t	g	l	i

(continued)

58   *Following Directions*

Name _____ Date _____

MULTIPLE-CHOICE TEST DIRECTIONS *(continued)*

> *Example:* Choose the best answer to complete this sentence:
>
> Abraham Lincoln was
>
> (a) a man   (b) the <u>16th president</u>   (c) tall and thin   (d) Nancy's son

1. Which one of these is not part of an automobile engine?
   (a) carburetor (b) spark plugs (c) valves (d) tires

2. *(Underline each incorrect answer.)* Some animals smaller than a mouse are:
   (a) horse (b) giraffe (c) ant (d) grizzly bear

3. *(Underline each answer that correctly completes the following sentence.)*
   To follow directions, you must
   (a) listen (b) concentrate (c) think (d) dance

4. *(Underline the correct answer.)* The following are examples of shapes:
   (a) rectangle (b) math (c) equation (d) computer

5. *(Underline the answer that incorrectly completes the following sentence.)*
   Some modern-day "monsters" that some people believe in are
   (a) Big Foot (b) Loch Ness Monster (c) Superman (d) ghosts and witches

6. A field of study that is not a branch of science is
   (a) biology (b) music (c) physics (d) geology

7. *(Underline the best answer(s) to complete this sentence.)*
   Following directions is a skill that can help you
   (a) at work (b) at school (c) at home (d) rarely, if ever

EXERCISE 23

TRUE-FALSE QUESTION DIRECTIONS

True-false questions look easy, but they can be very tricky. Just one word in the sentence can make the difference between a true statement and a false one.

Here are some hints for true-false questions.

> 1. Read the instructions. The teacher may ask you to use *T* or *F* for "true" or "false." You may be asked to write out the whole word. Or, you may be asked to use + or –. (These different systems are used because of confusion over the legibility of the *T* and *F*. To avoid arguments, teachers may have a fairly rigid system.)
>
> 2. If you think a sentence is true, read it again. If it is only partly true, it is false.
>
> 3. Pay attention to the word *not*. It will change the meaning of the sentence.
>
> 4. Look out for the words *never, always, all,* or *none*. They often make a sentence false because they are too restrictive.

Directions: Write TRUE or FALSE on the line before each sentence below.

_____ 1. True-false questions are always easy.

_____ 2. You never have to worry about true-false questions, since you have a 50-50 chance of getting it right.

_____ 3. A sentence that is only partially true is false.

_____ 4. Directions for true-false tests are always the same.

_____ 5. Objective questions ask for short, factual answers.

_____ 6. Examples of objective questions are multiple-choice, matching, true-false, fill-ins, and essays.

_____ 7. There is no point in planning your time when taking a test. Just see how it goes.

_____ 8. *Compare* and *contrast* mean the same thing.

_____ 9. Don't worry about directions in essay questions. Just start writing.

_____ 10. Fill-in tests require you to supply the answers.

MATCHING AND FILL-IN QUESTION DIRECTIONS

Matching

Matching questions ask you to match items in one column with items in a second column. Often, you will be matching words with their definitions.

Here are some hints for answering matching questions.

1. Read the instructions carefully. Be sure you know whether each choice is to be used only once or if it can be used many times.

2. Try to figure out the answer before you look down the matching column.

3. Work your way down the matching column, matching items you know first.

4. Mark off each answer as you use it. (You may not wish to do this if the answer can be used more than once.)

Directions: Match each word in column A with its definition in column B. Use each definition only once. Write the letter of the correct definition on the line before each word.

A

_____ true-false question
_____ fill-in question
_____ essay
_____ multiple-choice
_____ matching

B

(a) several choices are given
(b) answer true or false
(c) supply a short answer
(d) write a paragraph or more
(e) connect items in two columns

Fill-in Questions

These are also called **short-answer questions**. In these questions, you are to supply answers in your own words. The answers might be single words, full sentences, or phrases. Read the directions to be sure.

There are a few other helpful clues for this type of question: Know your material well. Read the directions carefully to be sure you are supplying the type of answer asked for.

Directions: Fill in one word to complete each sentence.

1. Fill-in questions are also called _____-answer questions.

2. Fill-ins may ask for one word or full _____.

3. In fill-ins, you supply the answers in your own _____.

EXERCISE 25

FIND THE MISTAKES

Directions: In this exercise, you are to proofread a sample student test. Read all the directions carefully. You will find nine places on the test where the student did not follow directions. List the nine errors on the lines on the next page.

Name _**Carl Netherton**_ ___ Date _____ Teacher _**Social Studies**___
     (Last, first, middle)

I. True-False. Write + on the line if the sentence is true. Write 0 if it is false.

**true**   1. Directions may be oral or written.

**false**   2. Hearing and listening are the same thing.

II. Matching. Write the letter of the phrase on the right that best describes each example on the left. You will use one letter more than once.

_**a**_ Teacher announces an assignment   (a) oral directions

_**b**_ Directions on a test   (b) written directions

_**c**_ Medicine label   (c) neither of these

III. Short Answer. In a single sentence, summarize the importance of following directions.
Following directions is a skill we'll need again and again. Both in school and at work it is important.

IV. Definitions. Write a definition of a "direction cue" in fewer than ten words.
A direction cue is a way teachers get your attention.

V. Tell whether the *italicized* word in each sentence is used correctly (C) or incorrectly (I).

Incorrect 1. An *antonym* is a word that means the same thing as another word.

Correct 2. To *outline* is to give the main points.

VI. Multiple Choice. Circle the letter of the correct answer.

1. A direction cue is
   (a) <u>an attention getter</u>
   (b) a traffic light
   (c) a road map
   (d) all of these

(continued)

FIND THE MISTAKES *(continued)*

The Errors:

1. _____
   _____

2. _____
   _____

3. _____
   _____

4. _____
   _____

5. _____
   _____

6. _____
   _____

7. _____
   _____

8. _____
   _____

9. _____
   _____

WRITING TEST QUESTIONS

Directions: Using a subject you are studying in class, prepare a short test on the material. Write directions and questions for each type of question listed below. Exchange papers with another student. Each of you is to follow the directions given. Then, give the papers back and see how well each of you followed the directions.

- **Multiple-choice:** Write directions and one question.

- **True-false:** Write directions and two questions.

- **Matching:** Write directions and two columns of four items each.

- **Fill-in:** Write directions and two questions.

- **Essay:** Write directions and one question.

EXERCISE 27

USING A STANDARDIZED ANSWER SHEET

On many types of tests (driver's license exams, civil service exams, college entrance exams, and even many school tests), you will use a standardized answer sheet. It is important that you follow the directions on these tests exactly. If you do not, you may not get credit for what you know. The directions in the box below are those found on most standardized answer sheets. Read and remember them as you complete the work on this page.

> Follow these directions for all work on this page: Mark only one answer for each item. Stray or additional marks may be counted as mistakes. Erase any errors completely. Make glossy black marks using a No. 2 pencil.

Directions: Look at the student answer sheet in the box below. On the line at the left of each row, write *correct* if the answer space in that row was marked correctly. If the answer space was not marked correctly, tell why not.

1. _____
2. _____
3. _____
4. _____
5. _____

Directions: Complete each statement below by circling the letter of the correct answer. Then mark the answer sheet on the right correctly.

6. When you listen to directions, you should (a) pay attention (b) take notes   (c) ask questions if you don't understand (d) all of these   (e) none of these

   6. A   B   C   D   E

7. To follow oral directions, you must first (a) read them carefully   (b) sit down (c) listen to them   (d) all of these   (e) none of these

   7. A   B   C   D   E

8. Listening means (a) the same as hearing   (b) paying attention to what you hear   (c) very little in following directions   (d) all of these   (e) none of these

   8. A   B   C   D   E

9. To get assignments right, you should (a) have an assignment notebook   (b) write down all your assignments (c) pay attention   (d) all of these   (e) none of these

   9. A   B   C   D   E

10. Taking notes is (a) a good way to remember things (b) only for people with poor memories (c) a waste of time   (d) all of these   (e) none of these

   10. A   B   C   D   E

USING DIRECTION CUES IN TEXTBOOKS

Overview

Nearly all textbooks contain direction cues which make it easier for the student to read and comprehend the material. The main direction cues are the chapter summary (or outline) and the boldface headings, which show the main ideas of the chapter.

Instructions

Exercise 28 consists of two pages. The first page contains information about reading textbooks using direction cues. This page may be assigned as silent reading, read aloud by the teacher as students follow along, or read aloud by students. The second page is to be completed as an independent student activity.

Answer Key

Exercise 28: Using Direction Cues in Textbooks

1. the beginning or end of the chapter

2. It tells you what the main ideas of the chapter will be. It alerts you to what is coming in the reading.

3. They are in larger, boldface print.

4. They give the main ideas.

5. pictures and other visual aids

6. five minutes or so

7. You will read more efficiently, since you know ahead of time what main ideas you are looking for.

8. Answers will vary.

Additional Activities

1. Bring in a variety of textbooks. Have pairs of students examine these and report to the class on the direction cues they find.

2. Discuss the direction cues in one of the textbooks used by your class.

USING DIRECTION CUES IN TEXTBOOKS

In Exercises 7 through 10, we learned that teachers often give direction cues to let you know when they are about to say something you should remember. Text-books also have direction cues. Learning how to recognize and follow these written direction cues can help you get more out of your textbooks.

Let's say you are asked to "read the next chapter in your textbook." If you're like most students, you sit down (hopefully with the radio and TV off) and read the chapter from start to finish. When you've finished reading, how much do you remember? If you're like most of us, not as much as you'd like.

Let's look at some ways to use direction cues to get those main ideas from your reading in an easier way.

The first direction cue in a chapter is the **chapter summary** or **chapter outline**. Usually, this is found at the beginning of the chapter. Sometimes, it is found at the end of the chapter. Read it carefully. It contains an overview of the important points the chapter will cover. By getting an overall picture of what you're about to read, you'll find your reading makes more sense.

The next direction cues in a chapter are the **section headings**, which are usually in larger, **boldface print**. Flip through the chapter. Read the headings. They are important direction cues which give you the main ideas of the different sections in the chapter.

While you're flipping through the chapter, notice the **pictures** and other **visual aids** (graphs, for example). These are more clues to the important points of the chapter.

Once you've done these things, you're ready to start reading. Your chapter overview should have taken you no more than five minutes or so. But, you've given yourself a big advantage as far as understanding what you're about to read.

As you read, pay attention again to the headings. Use each heading as a main idea. Then, make sure that what you read makes sense. When you finish reading, **reread** the chapter summary. Everything in it should now make sense. If you've missed a main idea mentioned in the summary, reread that part of the chapter.

(continued)

EXERCISE 28

USING DIRECTION CUES
IN TEXTBOOKS *(continued)*

1. In which two places is the chapter summary most often found?

2. How do you think reading the chapter summary before beginning the reading of a chapter can be helpful?

3. How can headings in a chapter be easily identified?

4. What is the purpose of headings in a textbook?

5. Name two other direction cues you might find in a textbook chapter.

6. How long do you think you should spend doing an overview of a chapter?

7. How do you think doing a chapter overview can save you time in the long run?

8. Examine one of your textbooks. Make a list of the direction cues you find in one of the chapters.

29: FOLLOWING INSTRUCTIONS TO MAKE A BOX
30: FOLLOWING DIRECTIONS TO MAKE CARAMEL POPCORN
31: MEDICINE LABEL INSTRUCTIONS
32: SOCIAL SECURITY CARD APPLICATION INSTRUCTIONS
33: JOB APPLICATION INSTRUCTIONS

Overview

There are endless applications for the skill of following directions in "real life." These exercises highlight just a few of these applications.

Answer Key

Exercise 29: Following Instructions to Make a Box

Check each student's box to make sure instructions were followed. You may wish to make additional copies of the pattern before beginning this exercise in case some of the boxes are ruined in the process.

Exercise 30: Following Directions to Make Caramel Popcorn

1. FALSE	9. TRUE
2. FALSE	10. FALSE
3. FALSE	11. FALSE
4. TRUE	12. FALSE
5. FALSE	13. TRUE
6. FALSE	14. TRUE
7. FALSE	15. FALSE
8. TRUE	16. TRUE

17. The popcorn scorches easily if it pops too long.

18. There is some danger in preparing the popcorn because both the popcorn and the caramel mixture get very hot.

19. Answers will vary, but no younger than 12 would be an appropriate answer.

Exercise 31: Medicine Label Instructions

Aspirin: 1. No 2. No 3. Yes 4. No 5. No

Queasy: 1. No 2. No 3. No 4. No 5. Yes

Exercise 32: Social Security Card Application Instructions

1. No
2. No
3. Yes
4. No
5. No
6. No
7. Yes
8. Yes

Check students' applications individually to see if they followed the directions.

Exercise 33: Job Application Instructions

1. Social Security card and birth certificate
2. No 3. No 4. No

Check job applications individually to see if students followed the directions.

Additional Activities

1. Obtain labels from various medicines. Make up questions about the directions.

2. Have each student bring a recipe to class. Have the student write five questions

about the directions in his or her recipe. Students may then exchange and answer each other's questions.

3. Save several newspaper sale ads. Write questions about the sales. (*Examples:* When does the sale start? Are *all* the shoes on sale?)

4. Obtain directions for using an electrical appliance (such as a blow-dryer). Write questions about the safety rules given in the directions.

5. Bring in a variety of clothing care labels. Write questions about the directions given on the labels for cleaning or washing the items.

6. Get some directions for a simple fix-it project such as repairing a lamp. Write questions about the directions.

7. Obtain various forms or job applications. Have students practice filling these out, following the directions carefully.

8. Get a book on origami or paper folding. Have students follow directions to make a project.

9. Bring in a variety of household products such as bleach, hairspray, and paint. Write questions about the directions for their use. Have students answer questions about a variety of the products.

FOLLOWING INSTRUCTIONS
TO MAKE A BOX

Directions: Read all instructions before you begin. You may wish to trace the box pattern onto another piece of paper before you cut. That way you can make more boxes later.

Here are the terms used in this project:

A **solid line** _____ means to cut.

A **dashed line** – – – – – – – – – – means to fold back.

Fold means to crease the paper sharply.

> Follow these steps to make a box.
> 1. Cut out the box along the solid lines.
> 2. Cut slits in corners 1 and 2.
> 3. Fold back on all the dashed lines.
> 4. Overlap the two *X*'s on corner 3. Do not make creases.
> 5. Slide corner 3 into slot 1.
> 6. Spread out the flap so the two *X*'s show again.
> 7. Overlap the two *X*'s on corner 4. Do not make creases.
> 8. Slide corner 4 into slot 2.
> 9. Spread out the flaps so the two *X*'s show again.

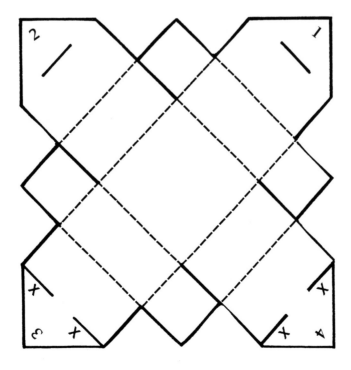

71   *Following Directions*

FOLLOWING DIRECTIONS TO MAKE CARAMEL POPCORN

Read the instructions for making microwave caramel popcorn. Then answer the questions that follow.

Instructions for Sam's Caramel Microwave Popcorn

1. Unfold the bag and place it in the middle of the microwave oven. Place the side marked "This Side Up" facing up. Do not put the foil pouch of caramel in the microwave.

2. Microwave the popcorn on high until popping slows to 2 or 3 seconds between pops. Popping time may be from 1 to 5 minutes. Overcooking may cause scorching. Do not leave microwave unattended while popping corn.

3. Remove bag from oven. Open top of bag by pulling diagonally on corners. Contents are very hot.

4. Remove caramel from foil pouch. Place caramel on top of popcorn in bag. Fold the top of the bag so it fits in microwave.

5. Heat on high for 1–2 minutes. Carefully remove bag from oven. Contents are very hot.

6. Keep bag tightly closed and shake well to spread caramel. Spread popcorn onto a cookie sheet and allow it to cool.

Satisfaction Guaranteed or Your Money Back.
Use Under Adult Supervision Only.

Write TRUE or FALSE on the line by each statement about making the caramel popcorn.

_____ 1. Put the bag and the foil caramel pouch in the microwave oven.

_____ 2. It doesn't matter which side of the bag is up.

_____ 3. Pop the corn on medium power.

_____ 4. Stop the microwave when there are 2–3 seconds between pops.

_____ 5. The popcorn will take 5 minutes to pop.

(continued)

         Following Directions

Name _____ Date _____

FOLLOW THE DIRECTIONS
TO MAKE CARAMEL POPCORN *(continued)*

_____ 6. Overcooking will dry out the popcorn.

_____ 7. Cut the popcorn bag open with scissors.

_____ 8. Remove the caramel from its pouch and place it on top of the popcorn.

_____ 9. Fold the top of the bag shut.

_____ 10. Lay the bag on its side and place it in the microwave oven.

_____ 11. Heat the popcorn and caramel on high for 1 to 5 minutes.

_____ 12. The popcorn is ready to eat when you first take it out of the oven.

_____ 13. Shake the popcorn to spread the caramel.

_____ 14. Spread the popcorn on a cookie sheet and let it cool.

_____ 15. You could also make this popcorn in a regular oven.

_____ 16. If you don't like this popcorn, you can get a refund.

What Do You Think?

17. Why do you think the directions say not to leave the microwave unattended while popping corn?

18. Why do you think the package says "Use Under Adult Supervision Only"?

19. How old do you think a person should be to prepare this product safely on his or her own?

Name _____   Date _____

EXERCISE 31

MEDICINE LABEL INSTRUCTIONS

Directions: Read labels A and B. Then read what some people did with the medicine. Decide if each person followed the directions. Write *Yes* or *No* on the line by each question.

A.

Aspirin
Dosage: Adults: 2 tablets every 4 hours as needed.
Do not exceed 8 tablets in 24 hours unless told to do so by physician.
Children ages 6–12: 1 tablet every 4 hours.
Children under 6: Consult physician.
If you are taking other medication, consult physician before taking aspirin.

_____ 1. Lucy gave aspirin to her teething baby.

_____ 2. Shelley took aspirin and a cold medicine at the same time before calling the doctor.

_____ 3. Jacob took eight aspirin in a day, but he still had a headache. So he checked with his doctor.

_____ 4. Matt took aspirin at 10:00 A.M. He took another dose at noon.

_____ 5. Mrs. Young gave her five-year-old two tablets every four hours as needed.

B. _____ 1. Mr. Foster gave his three-year-old son two teaspoons of Queasy for diarrhea.

_____ 2. Mrs. Chan decided to take Queasy for her morning sickness while she was pregnant.

_____ 3. Jo Lynn took Queasy and aspirin for the flu. When her ears began to ring, she made an appointment with her ear doctor right away.

_____ 4. Luis, age four, was given Queasy for his high fever and diarrhea for three days. His mother decided to buy new medicines.

_____ 5. Mrs. Youngblood gave Mary, age four, one teaspoon of Queasy at these times: 8:00, 9:00, 10:00, 11:00, 12:00, 1:00, 2:00, and 3:00. Finally, Mary seemed to be better.

Queasy Upset Stomach Medicine
Directions:
Adults: 2 tablespoons
Children: 10–14: 4 teaspoons
6–10: 2 teaspoons
3–6: 1 teaspoon
Repeat above dosage every $\frac{1}{2}$ to 1 hour if needed until 8 doses are taken.
Caution: If taken with aspirin and ringing of ears occurs, discontinue use.
If pregnant or nursing, consult physician before using this product.
If diarrhea and high fever are present for more than 2 days, consult physician.
For relief of upset stomach and diarrhea.

Following Directions

SOCIAL SECURITY CARD
APPLICATION INSTRUCTIONS

Directions: Look carefully at the Social Security card application below. Then, read the sentences below the application. Write *Yes* on the line in front of the sentence if that person followed the directions. Write *No* if the person did not. After you have answered the questions, fill in the application as if you were applying for a Social Security card.

ID: CN: DO:	⌐ DO NOT WRITE IN THE ABOVE SPACE ⌐

APPLICATION FOR A SOCIAL SECURITY NUMBER.
See Instructions on Back.   Print in Black or Dark Blue Ink or Use Typewriter.

1 Print FULL NAME YOU WILL USE IN WORK OR BUSINESS   (First Name)   (Middle Name or Initial—if none, draw line _____)   (Last Name)

2 Print FULL NAME GIVEN YOU AT BIRTH   **6** YOUR DATE OF BIRTH   (Month) (Day) (Year)

3 PLACE OF BIRTH   (City)   (County if known)   (State)   **7** YOUR PRESENT AGE *(Age on last birthday)*

4 MOTHER'S FULL NAME AT HER BIRTH *(Her maiden name)*   **8** YOUR SEX   MALE ☐   FEMALE ☐

5 FATHER'S FULL NAME *(Regardless of whether living or dead)*   **9** YOUR COLOR OR RACE   WHITE ☐   NEGRO ☐   OTHER ☐

10 HAVE YOU EVER BEFORE APPLIED FOR OR HAD A UNITED STATES SOCIAL SECURITY, RAILROAD, OR TAX ACCOUNT NUMBER?   NO ☐   DON'T KNOW ☐   YES ☐   (If "Yes" Print **State** in which you applied and **Date** you applied and **Social Security Number** if known)

11 YOUR MAILING ADDRESS   (Number and Street, Apt. No., P.O. Box, or Rural Route)   (City)   (State)   (Zip Code)

12 TODAY'S DATE   **14** NOTICE: Whoever, with intent to falsify his or someone else's true identity, wilfully furnishes or causes to be furnished false information in applying for a social security number, is subject to a fine of not more than $1,000 or imprisonment for up to 1 year, or both.

13 TELEPHONE NUMBER   Sign YOUR NAME HERE *(Do Not Print)*

DHEW Social Security Administration
Form **SS–5**   ☐ RESCREEN   ☐ ASSIGN   ☐ DUP ISSUED   Return completed application to nearest SOCIAL SECURITY ADMINISTRATION OFFICE

_____ 1. Joey filled out his form with a No. 2 pencil.

_____ 2. Elizabeth does not have a middle name. So she wrote *None* on line 1 in the space for a middle name.

_____ 3. Toh carefully printed his full name on line 2.

_____ 4. Sally Wilson wrote her mother's name, "Mrs. Ruth Wilson," on line 4.

_____ 5. Ed's father died, so he left line 5 blank.

_____ 6. Leon will be 16 next week. So he wrote *16* on line 7.

_____ 7. Jean sent her completed application to the Social Security Administration Office in her town.

_____ 8. Drew needed more instructions on how to fill out the form. So, he turned the application over and read the instructions on the back.

EXERCISE 33

JOB APPLICATION INSTRUCTIONS

Directions: Read the boxed "Instructions to Job Applicants" and answer the questions to the right. Then fill in the job application using your own information. Follow all directions carefully.

WAGNER'S DEPARTMENT STORE
Instructions to Job Applicants

Applications will be taken between 8 A.M. and 5 P.M. Monday–Friday, and 8 A.M. to 12 P.M. Saturday. Bring your Social Security card and birth certificate when you apply. If you are applying for work in the delivery section, you must bring your driver's license. After we have looked over your completed application, we may phone you at home to set up an interview time.

---

1. What papers must all applicants bring?

2. Will salesperson applicants need to have a driver's license?

3. Will everyone who applies be asked to come for an interview?

4. Is 3:30 on Saturday a good time to bring back your completed application?

Job Application: Print or type all information.

Today's date _____ Social Security no. _____

Name _____ Present age _____
           Last   *First*   *Middle*

Address _____
        No. and Street   *City*   *State*   *Zip*

Phone no. _____ Date of birth _____

Height _____ Weight _____ Married _____ Single _____ Divorced _____

No. of children _____ Are you a United States citizen? _____

Name and address of
last school attended _____ Dates _____

Circle last year completed Grade 5 6 7 8 H.S. 1 2 3 4 Other 1 2 3 4

Special training and skills _____

WORK HISTORY: List below your last 2 employers; start with last one first.

Dates Worked	Name and Address of Employer	Position	Reason for Leaving

In case of emergency, notify _____
                Name   *Phone*

REFERENCES: Give the names of 2 persons, not relatives, who have known you at least 1 year.

Name	Address	Occupation	Phone

I declare that all information on this form is correct. _____
                                          (signature)